PREFACE

The data science can be defined as the convergence of Computer Science, programming, mathematical modeling, data analytics, academic expertise, traditional AI research, and applying the statistical techniques through scientific programming tools such as Python, R, TensorFlow, Java, on an ecosystem of SQL, NoSQL, GraphDB, streaming computing platforms such as Apache Spark, Apache Kafka, Apache Storm, Apache Nifi, Apache Flink, Apache Geode, and linked data to extract new knowledge discovery through data patterns and provide new insights from distributed computing platform from the tsunami of big data. Though, many times it is possible to define the statistical language models, it's difficult to implement through object-oriented programming languages. Therefore, it is critical to wear the hats of an advanced programmer, infrastructure architect to provide web scale performance with in-memory computing and apply traditional research with machine learning and deep learning algorithms to create novel architectures unique to each enterprise and avoid one-size fits all approach. Real-time analysis is all the rage in the data science industry. Therefore, leveraging in-memory computing ecosystems can provide faster execution results to the corporations.

Onalytica a company founded in 2009 provides global influencer software powered by big data and predictive analytics, real-time market intelligence for influencer identification in Machine Learning, Deep Learning, Data Science, IoT, SAP, Cloud Computing, Distributed Computing, Networks, and HPC, Analytics. This book is a gist of the interview held by Joe Fields from Onalytica with me, about my industrial expertise in data science, machine learning, Deep Learning, Data Science, IoT, SAP, Cloud Computing, Distributed Computing, Networks, and HPC, Analytics, predictions, the current state of data science, GitHub trends, and industrial trends for the future on these topics.

TABLE OF CONTENTS

What are going to be the key developments in the industry in the next 12 months?

    Machine Learning

    Deep Learning

    Data Science

    Cloud Computing, Distributed Computing, and HPC

    Definition of problem statement and scope

    Data collection

    Exploratory data analysis

    Development of prediction models

    Deployment of the model

    Azure Machine Learning

    Tableau

    SAP BusinessObjects BI

    QlikView

    Healthcare data privacy and consolidation of big data

    Optimization through efficiency

    Improved ROI

    Customer experience

    Improved healthcare

    Elimination of medical errors

    Key performance indicators

If a brand wanted to work with you, which activities would you be most interested in collaborating on?

What would be the best way for a brand to contact you?

REFERENCES

Bio

Dr. Ganapathi Pulipaka is the CEO, Chief Data Officer, Chief Data Scientist, and SAP Technical Lead of DeepSingularity LLC, a premier SAP and artificial intelligence consulting firm. He is also a PostDoc Research Scholar in Computer Science Engineering in Big Data Analytics, Machine Learning, Robotics, IoT, Artificial Intelligence as part of Doctor of Computer Science program from Colorado Technical University, CO with another PhD in Data Analytics, Information Systems, and Enterprise Resource Management, California University, Irvine, CA.

A technology leader in artificial intelligence, SAP development, and solution architecture. A project/program manager for application development of SAP systems, machine learning, deep learning systems, application development management, basis, infrastructure, and consulting delivery services offering expertise in delivery execution and executive interaction. Experienced implementing ASAP, Agile, Agile ASAP 8, HANA ASAP 8, Activate, Prince2, SCRUM, and Waterfall SDLC project methodologies. Implemented multiple SAP programs/projects managing a team size of 60+ members, managing budget more than $5M to $10M with SAP backend databases of Oracle, IBM DB2, Sybase, Informix, MS SQL server on Mac OS and Linux environments.

Background is in Computer Science with a professional skillset and two decades of management and hands-on development experience in Machine Learning in TensorFlow, Python, and R, Deep Learning in TensorFlow, Python, and R, SAP ABAP S/4 HANA 1609, SAP S/4 H HANA 1710, Big Data, IaaS, IoT, Data Science, Apache Hadoop, Apache Kafka, Apache Spark, Apache Storm, Apache Flink, SQL, NoSQL, Tableau, PowerBI, Mathematics, Data Mining, Statistical Framework, SIEM, SAP, SAP ERP/ECC 6.0 NetWeaver Portals, SAP PLM, cProjects, R/3, BW, SRM 5.0, CRM 7.4, 7.3, 7.2, 7.1, 7.0, Java, C, C++, VC++, SAP CRM-IPM, SAP CRM-Service management, SAP CRM-Banking, SAP PLM Web UI 7.47, xRPM, SCM 7.1 APO, DP, SNP, SNC, FSCM, FSCD, SCEM, EDI. CRM ABAP/OO, ABAP, CRM Web UI/BOL/GENIL/ABAP Objects, SAP Netweaver Gateway (OData), SAP Mobility, SAP Fiori, Information Security, CyberSecurity, Governance, Risk Controls, and Compliance, SAP Fiori HANA, ABAP Webdynpros, BSPs, EDI/ALE, CRM Middleware, CRM Workflow, JavaScript, SAP KW 7.3 SAP Content server, SAP TREX Server, SAP KPro, SAP PI (PO), SAP BPC, Script logics, Azure, SAP BPM, SAP UI5, SAP BRM, Unix, Linux, macOS, and always looking for patterns in data and performing extractions to provide new meanings and insights through algorithms and analytics.

- Design, develop, and deploy machine learning and deep learning applications to solve the real-world problems in natural language processing, speech recognition, text to speech, and speech to text analytics.
- Experience in data exploration, data preparation, applying supervised and unsupervised machine learning algorithms, machine learning model training, machine learning model evaluation, predictive analytics, bio-inspired algorithms, genetic algorithms, and natural language processing.
- Building recommendation systems and applying algorithms for anomaly detection in the financial industry.
- Deep reinforcement learning algorithms for robotics and IoT.
- Applying convolutional neural networks, recurrent neural networks, and long-term short memory with deep learning techniques to solve various conundrums.

- Developed number of machine learning and deep learning programs applying various algorithms and published articles with architecture and practical project implementations on medium.com, data driven investor, gppulipaka.org, deepsingularity.io, and LinkedIn.

- Experience with Python, TensorFlow, Caffe, Theano, Keras, Java, and R Programming languages implementing stacked auto encoders, backpropagation, perceptron, Restricted Boltzmann machines, and Deep Belief Networks.
- Interested in developing algorithms for biology, drug discovery in healthcare, utilities, energy, customer services, predictive maintenance applications and analytics in aerospace, and developing algorithms to run autonomous vehicles.
- Experience in multiple IoT platforms.

Location: Los Angeles, CA, USA

Key Topics:

- Machine Learning
- Deep Learning
- Data Science
- IoT
- SAP
- Cloud Computing, Distributed Computing, Networks, and HPC
- Analytics

Social Channels:

Twitter: @gp_pulipaka

LinkedIn: https://www.linkedin.com/in/dr-ganapathi-pulipaka-56417a2/

LinkedIn blogs: https://www.linkedin.com/in/dr-ganapathi-pulipaka-56417a2/detail/recent-activity/posts/

Blogs at www.gppulipaka.org http://gppulipaka.org/big-data-analytics

Blogs at www.deepsingularity.io under blogs section

I'm also a writer at http://www.datadriveninvestor.com/ where I share my practical data science, machine learning, IoT, analytics, and deep learning project implementations with Github repositories.

I contribute to medium a number of data science, analytics, SQL, NoSQL, Hadoop, IoT, machine learning, and deep learning articles at https://medium.com/

Facebook Public page: https://www.facebook.com/ganapathipulipaka/

Github code repositories: https://github.com/GPSingularity

Instagram: No account

How did you get to become an expert in Data Science?

The field of Computer Science Engineering has contributed significantly for the development of various mathematical models and algorithms since the inception of earlier Konrad Zuse programmable computers. Aerospace, high-speed trains, and automotive industries perform potential analysis with computational fluid dynamics. A number of pharmaceutical companies have been revolutionizing the field of drug discovery through high-performance computing machines on data science platforms. Proove Nexus platform created 28 billion data points for world's largest DNA pain bank and big data chronic dataset with 100,000 specimens. Quantum chemistry, quantum computing, energy industry, utilities, industrial manufacturing, and life science industries leverage novel applications to harness the power of big data. According to IDC, big data and data analytics will continue to grow to $210 billion by 2020. High-performance computing systems tend to move towards exascale. Approximately a supercomputing exascale machine alone consumes $2.5 b USD energy every year in 2010. The supercomputing machines are created with processors that double up their processing capabilities exponentially breaking down Moore's Law with mathematical models and algorithms. Attending or organizing Hackathons and winning AI programming competitions is entirely different from building and deploying large-scale enterprise scale AI systems. When I was 16 years old, I assembled a computer on my own including operating system and software installation. At this stage, already as a freelance programmer while still studying at college, I developed enterprise grade air traffic control system for Air Force Academy in C and C++ and received commendations and a certificate from Air Wing Commander. I continued to develop a vast number of commercial projects for a large number of companies at this age in C, C++, VC++, VB, and Java with Oracle database. Some of the major clients include State Electricity Board. Some of these companies had vast number of databases and data sources scattered throughout the organization on a number of systems. Independently I was able to wrangle all this data, preprocess it, and program it through algorithms and build predictive analytics with probability modeling, statistics, and mathematics to provide new insights and predictive analytics into their systems with high performing analytics before the birth of the term *data science*. Moving forward, I ended up with PostDoc in Computer Science Engineering, Machine Learning, Big Data Analytics with GPA 4.00 out of 4.00 as part of Doctor of Computer Science program from Colorado Technical University, Colorado Springs, CO and another PhD in Business Administration in Data Analytics, Information Systems, and Enterprise Resource Management with GPA 4.00 out of 4.00 from California University, Irvine, CA. Here my academic dissertation was *SAP HANA and In-Memory Computing to resolve the biggest business conundrums*. My book Big Data Appliances for In-Memory Computing – A Real World Research Guide for Corporations to Tame and Wrangle their data is an extended version of the dissertation looking from an enterprise lens. My PostDoc Dissertation *Deep Learning Frameworks in High Performance Computing Environments* is currently in publication with an International Research Journal. I worked for Big 4 technical consulting giants Capgemini and Deloitte both generated $15 billion and $38.8 billion annually in 2017 with pure consulting experience and 28 production deployment projects. With a vast experience of couple of decades in dealing with data I worked for fortune 100 corporations with heterogeneous business processes in processing extreme-scale data for Aerospace, Energy, Utilities, Retail, High-tech, life sciences, healthcare, chemical industry, FDA regulated corporations, banking, media and entertainment, service, manufacturing, and financial services.

Back in the day, my international career began in 2000 as a programmer tuning terabytes of data for off-the-charts dynamic performance of the systems at an energy company. In the world of SAP scaling and deploying terabyte systems was an everyday phenomenon couple of decades ago, while for corporations without SAP enterprise systems, data at this scale is just unheard. Some of the clients I implemented projects have large-scale data warehouses that require extensive data ingestion, data processing, data analytics, and programming.

What areas of the Data Science are you most passionate about?

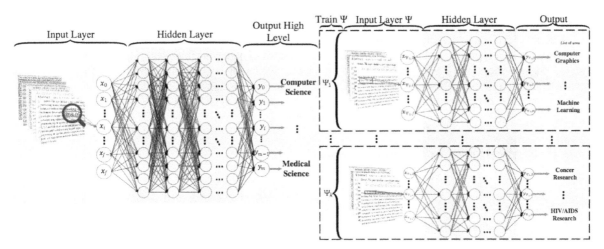

Fig. 1: HDLTex: Hierarchical Deep Learning for Text Classification. This is our Deep Neural Network (DNN) approach for text classification. The left figure depicts the parent-level of our model, and the right figure depicts child-level models defined by Ψ_i as input documents in the parent level.

I'm passionate about AI research, web-scale data science, and programming. In the year of 2014 alone, 28K+ peer-reviewed journals published 2.5M+ research articles. The rate of publication is exponentially accelerating. Supervised methods such as support vector machines, neural nets, Naïve Bayes, and few other ensemble methods were the primary sources of handling document classification. In the field of Computer Science, text classification and text mining require advanced processing techniques. The organizations have been experiencing degraded performance with the implementation of supervised machine learning techniques for document classification and retrieval. Novel techniques with deep neural networks and hierarchical deep learning provide a stack of levels of document hierarchies for faster processing of the unlabeled documents. Researching the new papers and reproducing the code to prove the work stated in the paper is my passion.

A large number of corporations are jumping on the bandwagon of artificial intelligence. Every corporation is involved in leveraging big data analytics to a larger extent in a distributed cloud computing environment or on-premise servers running machine learning and deep learning algorithms fueled mainly by three trends Algorithm economy, Data Flywheels, and artificial intelligence in a distributed cloud environment. In a recent Artificial Intelligence and Machine Learning Summit held in Seattle, WA trends were discussed on building the smarter artificial intelligence applications. The Summit emphasized building machine learning models that can be applied to a number of industries across the globe such as manufacturing, healthcare, retail, chemicals, aerospace, utilities, energy, pharmaceuticals, and semiconductors. The machine learning models in the distributed computing environment can aid the organizations to analyze large-scale data flowing from a number of disparate channels as continuous streams to produce instant results without having to invest in high-cost infrastructure to meet the economies of scale.

Data Flywheels

The big data is generated in the digital universe on the brink of Moore's Law. Every year the data is getting doubled and exponentially multiplying. The cost of storing the data is declining in a similar fashion. The ability of such large-scale big data is contributing to the creation of better machine learning models. Every corporation from their Data Flywheel can create sustainable machine learning models providing a greater customer experience for algorithmic economy. Tesla has gathered around 1.3 billion miles of autonomous data. The data collected can provide the ultimate basis for autonomous vehicles to be released in 2018.

The rise of algorithmic economy

The data deluge in the world can be leveraged through big data analytics tools with artificial intelligence to scale the business operations like never seen before. Algorithms will drive the businesses. This is what leads to an intelligence economy driven by algorithms. The dawn of intelligence economy powered by business intelligence and artificial intelligence has a huge impact on the big data analytics. The algorithmic economy is building a collaborative environment for researchers, machine learning experts, and corporations to build the intelligent algorithms at scale in walk of the business.

Distributed machine intelligence

The machine intelligence of algorithms is now distributed in a cloud-computing environment and will aid the organizations in future to discover valuable insights and perform several operations through APIs. Organizations are mass-manufacturing algorithms since it meets economies of scale in a distributed environment. Artificial intelligence is the new inferno for powering AI winter (that lasted from 1990s through 2010s) with the machine intelligence platforms through machine learning to rapidly prototype and deploy in production from sandboxes. A number of open-source machine learning and deep learning platforms have been released in the recent times such as TensorFlow by Google, Caffe by University of Berkeley, NLTK (Natural Language Tookit) by University of Pennsylvania for natural language processing, Scikit-learn machine learning library for Python, a number of R packages for deep learning and machine learning, Theano a numerical computation library for Python, Torch a platform for developing machine learning and deep learning with an underlying C implementation.

Artificial intelligence has huge impact on big data as they revolutionized several industries in the world the way they solve the unsolvable conundrums. Several machine learning algorithms contribute to the big data field through artificial intelligence. These can be classified into two categories. The first group of algorithms learns the existing datasets through training technique and the second group of machine learning algorithms can be categorized as clustering techniques that find similarity among multiple datasets and groups of datasets.

The most popular machine learning algorithm packages in R for code implementation are as follows:

- E1071: This package can be leveraged for random Fourier transformations, support vector machines, clustering, and a number of unsupervised and supervised algorithms.
- randomForest: For the implementation of regression and classification conundrums, this package can be installed with randomForest algorithms.

- Arules: A number of association rules algorithms can be implemented from this R package.
- Caret: A number of machine learning algorithms are rolled out in this R package for resolving classification and regression type of problems.
- Recommenderlab: Many corporations in today's world have implemented recommendation engines and systems for best customer experience.
- Recommenderlab R package delivers a number of features for implementation of the code.
- H2O: This R package is developed by H2O.ai Corporation that can be implemented for scalable and faster processing for deep learning and gradient boosting.
- Rpart: This R package can be implemented for data partitioning recursively or building the decision trees.
- Nnet: This R package can be implemented for deep learning leveraging the neural networks.

Web-scale data science

The evolution of web from Web 1.0 to Web 5.0 in the last few decades has introduced new capabilities and sources that contributed to the creation of massive volumes of big data. The semantics of World Wide Web and Internet are synonymous. However, the functionality of World Wide Web is different, as it creates a social ecosystem through the technology powered by the Web-scale complex networks. The World Wide Web provides the network systems to enable humans to interact socially and collaborate through cognitive communication. Tim Burners-Lee conceived the idea of World Wide Web in 1989. In the last few decades, the World Wide Web has evolved from Web 1.0 to Web 5.0 in many significant ways.

Web 1.0

Construction of Web 1.0 was to provide the cognitive power to the humans, primarily for corporations to broadcast their information through the new net of technology. This was a catalyst-broadcasting medium contrasted with the conventional paper-based information transmission. The Web was mostly built with the static HTML display of the content and with no interaction or updates performed on the data flowing through the web. It provided some search functionalities. The content contribution had limited distribution and participation. The objective of constructing Web 1.0 was to build a singular UDI (Universal Document Identifier) that can store large-scale data in a single document. Web 1.0 was primarily static with read-only functionality. Corporations led the Web 1.0 revolution as a broadcasting platform to present all of their business features for the larger audience.

The websites lacked responsive design to provide any interactive features, mostly similar to a newspaper ad or a brochure with business information. The content on the web was constant and retained for long periods without any updates. Web 1.0 was built on the protocols of HTTP (Hypertext Transfer Protocol), HTML (Hypertext markup language), and URI (Universal Resource Identifier). The Web 1.0 also contained the latest protocols such as XHTML, XML, ASP, CSS, CGI, JSP, PERL client-side scripting, VBScript, and JavaScript. The architecture was based on a client-server architecture where web client served as the web browser on the World Wide Web sending the request to Web service to receive a response back to the web client.

The Web 1.0 lasted for a long time from 1989 through 2005. The web did not support mass production of publications. It was mostly for a particular business corporation with specific display of content pooling Uniform Resource Identifiers (URIs). The Webmaster is the administrator for Web 1.0 and connects all the hyperlinks to the content published. Frameset has been heavily leveraged in Web 1.0. Only humans could interpret the data content from Web 1.0 and there were no machine intelligence, machine-to-machine, human-to-machine communication protocols.

Web 2.0

The conceptual framework behind Web 2.0 was to power the World Wide Web with communication networks. The advent of Web 2.0 was conceived by Dale Dougherty in 2004. For the first time, the Web 2.0 introduced the write functionality of the data along with read functionality. The data aggregation was pooled from a massive number of crowds and the construct of the data allowed people to interact with each other based on their shared interests. O'Reilly conducted a conference on the future of the web. The conference introduced a new concept of read-write functionality on the web. The idea behind Web 2.0 introduced collaborative networks and interactions among the humans provisioning distributed contributions over large-scale networks and moved away from static HTML websites that only served as portals of information. Several media companies had shown interest in the conference to distribute their data and allow the public to contribute and participate in social technology networks. Web 2.0 aided as knowledge hubs for the public. The web was not static anymore.

Web 2.0 brought collective intelligence and collaboration from the static web content display models, thus allowing the people to create colossal amounts of big data on the web. The era of Web 2.0 has seen new innovatory technologies to power the web and aggregate the data from different networks. The rise of Web 2.0 has introduced an array of social networking technologies such as Twitter, Facebook, and videos sharing site YouTube, knowledge-based sites such as Wikipedia. These sites have rapidly accumulated the data through HTML via HTTP services with URIs. The emphasis has shifted from business corporations broadcasting their data through information brochure format static HTML content display to building social communities that are content aggregators. The technology advanced from client-server networks to peer-to-peer networks. New RSS feeds (Really Simple Syndication) have allowed the public to become their own content aggregators. The webmasters were no more the owners of the business websites. The public was able to contribute, collaborate and share the content. The speed of the networks accelerated from dialup connection to broadband, thus tremendously allowing the public to create gargantuan amounts of data. The web has evolved from static information portal to a dynamic platform. New form of data was generated enormously through blogs and articles in the form of text and video. The rise of the Wikis has created knowledge hubs aggregating colossal volumes of data on the web.

Web 3.0

Web 3.0 was built keeping in view of the collaboration among the humans. The focus was on automation of tasks performed by the human with machine intelligence and machine interpreted semantics. The rise of the social networking communities can be largely contributed to Web 3.0 revolution for collaboration between humans and machines. John Markoff coined the term Web 3.0 sometime around 2006. Web 3.0 was prominently known as semantic web. The web was built with smart and intelligent applications that allowed individuals to contribute and read the content. Web 3.0 created new types of data artifacts such as encyclopedias, online books, health care research data, geospatial GIS information. The Web 3.0 allowed execution of the content. The melding of Unicode and URI represented a unique international character set written in any language as unique identifiers for the data. The advent of XML (Extensible markup language) allowed transmission of the information between various platforms. Web 4.0 is a multi-layered semantic web with the framework components such as URI, Unicode, XML, RDF schema, RDF, ontology, proof, and unifying logic.

Web 4.0

The construction of Web 4.0 was for integration of networks and transmission of the data with intelligent interactions with the coalition of human and machine intelligence. The Web 4.0 introduced machine intelligence, operational intelligence, and generated huge amounts of machine-to-human, and human-to-machine data. Websites like Amazon has learnt the habits of visitors and provided recommendations on the product purchases. The web has spread out to various devices such as smart tablets and smart phones. The technology advancements of the billions of transistors development on a single silicon chip has pushed the envelope of web to power the nanotechnology devices for healthcare and improvement of performance. The data deluge increased to petabytes.

Web 5.0

Web 5.0 is the future of the World Wide Web also dubbed *Brain-Net*. It is currently work-in-progress and aimed to bring a revolution of all times where people can interact by sharing emotions, memories, and experiences. It is popularized as the Symbionet Web with the concepts of communication through SmartCommunicators and brain. It is considered to be a 3D World Wide Web.

Data science powers web. Most of the big data generates from the web. Corporations powered by web-technologies such as Google processes around 3.5 billion requests per day and currently estimated to store 10 exabytes of the data. Google and Microsoft put together have one million servers to process the big data coming from the web. Facebook processes around 500 terabytes of data per day. According to an estimate from the research giant IDC by 2020, the world will generate a massive amount of 40 zettabytes of data by 2020. By 2012, the world has produced colossal amounts of 500 exabytes from the World Wide Web alone. The future growth pattern of big data shows that big data doubles up every two years and grows 50-fold from 2010 through 2020 showing the signs of technology singularity with law of exponential returns.

As the volume of the big data grows tremendously through the web, there are several impacts on the processing engines of big data coming from the web. The performance bottlenecks can stem from the following factors:

- Tremendous workloads surpassing the DRAM allocations on the servers
- The amount of time spent on running the SQL and NoSQL queries
- Deadlocks on the database performing write operations with parallel computing operations on distributed clusters
- The scalability issues to retrieve large amounts of data while connecting multiple databases to retrieve the records
- Multiple read or write operations on a shared hard disk drive that can result in power outages or heat death
- Complex processing of unstructured big data from the web requires big data tools such as Apache Hadoop, Cloudera, HortonWorks, and MapR technologies through programming such as Java. The programming can run into performance bottlenecks due to multithreaded processing, parallel computing, and distributed computing
- Complex event processing with several dependencies between the events
- The performance bottlenecks in the programming can also arise due to the lack of best practices in the programming due to lack of scalability in the program
- The complex processing of algorithmic programming that requires intensive calculations
- Accessing conventional disk-based databases
- Buffer overflows on Linux, Unix, macOS, and other operating systems
- Allocation of non-scalable buffer sizes for TCP protocols
- Lack of memcached techniques
- Lack of optimization of cache for the web
- Network bandwidth I/O bottlenecks and L1 and L2 caches
- Local overloads of data on the CPUs
- Lack of bandwidth in the packet sizes over the network

As the big data continues to grow through the web, the challenges increased potentially to transfer the data over the web due to the sheer volume size of the big data in the recent times. The trend continued for the labs engaged in biomedical research. Because, it is highly cost-intensive and time-intensive with the risk of potential performance bottlenecks; these research labs from Boston and Seattle chose to ship physically the data hard drives. This new requirement of data in transit arose purely due to the network bandwidth and latency constraints through the web. The data from the medical research labs contain tumor images sizing from 3 gigabytes to 10 gigabytes. As there are 1000s of cancer tumor samples, the big data size grows tremendously. One of the most common performance bottlenecks experienced while transferring the big data over the computer network on the web is congestion avoidance. The data transfers rate and efficiency over the network depend on the amount of data supplied vs. the data demanded by the network. If the data supply exceeds the demand, the network starts experiencing dropped packets and creates a delayed network path which can take very long time to transfer the packets of big data over the network. The algorithm of congestion avoidance might work well in local area network environments, but on global computing networks or wide area networks, it's a different strategy altogether. The distance between source of data origin and the destination of the data transmission is directly proportional to the data speed of the network.

IBM recently acquired Aspera, that transmits the data through fasp protocol that can transfer the data over the network and cloud of clouds with ultra-blazing speeds to handle the performance bottlenecks.

Programming

Programming has been my passion for all through my life processing large-scale big data. Design patterns in object-oriented programming can be implemented on several projects. I see patterns everywhere, just like mathematical numbers, there's a pattern of code to everything in the universe. Programming is a way of visualizing the universe through code design patterns. It's also important to maintain high quality code on rapid paced implementation projects to give a high success rate to the project. An empirical research study has been conducted in October 2017 on a large-scale Github dataset that contains 17 programming languages, 728 projects, 63 million source lines of code, 1.5 million commits, with 29,000 authors to evaluate the effect of programming languages on the quality of the software code. Machine learning techniques such as multiple regression models constructed with natural language processing (Latent Dirichlet Allocation), and text analytics to unravel the data visualizations of the code quality. Based on the empirical evidence through Google's BigQuery, several factors associated with the quality of the code assessed such as size of the code, team size, age, and maturity levels. The code study subjects included the programming languages such as C, C++, C#, Objective-C, Go, Java, JavaScript, TypeScript, Ruby, Php, Python, Perl, Clojure, Erlang, Haskell, and Scala. The research study aimed to determine if some programming languages are more prone-defect than other programming languages. The results have shown that projects developed in C, C++, Objective-C, Php, and Python have a greater number of defects associated in stark contrast to Clojure, Haskell, Ruby, and Scala that have shown minimum number of defect commits on Github. Considering it's a large-scale study with a massive Github dataset with multiple dimensions of data, the empirical evidence has been proven.

Which Data Science influencers influence you?

I'm influenced by data science research papers from arXiv, bioRxiv, ACM Digital Library, IEEE Explore Library, Science Direct, Github, ProQuest database, Emerald Engineering publications, SAGE Journals, Springer, Safari Books Online, and Books 24 x 7. ProQuest database consists a number of dissertations on artificial intelligence. These are the sources of my data science inspiration as they have credible citations and sources as references. There's a misconception in the industry that these papers are purely in academic nature. However, a majority of these papers have Github repositories with code to reproduce the results. The aspiring data scientists are highly encouraged to try this out. Occasionally I stumble upon some good blogs and articles written by people whose data can be verified through an architecture reference and verification system that I adapted. Other than that I write my own blogs and articles to share with the data science community. Twitter scraping, web scraping from a single source of inspiration, and closed-access communities can cripple down the data science community as a) the net neutrality decreases due to opinionated articles written to support a set of people b) accuracy is hard to verify as most of these articles are not checked for plagiarism and not checked with references and in-text citations. Therefore, the quality increases when accessing multiple academic journals, books, and eBooks as these are checked for plagiarism and originality. Therefore, my Twitter timeline is the best way of getting hold of a wide range of data science and AI, IoT (net neutrality) topics to benefit enterprises and data science entrepreneuring individuals and aspiring data scientists.

Outside of the Data Science who else influences you?

I'm influenced by my parents.

How would you describe your offline influence?

I'm a public keynote speaker and bestselling author. My book *Big Data Appliances for In-Memory Computing: A Real-World Research Guide for Corporations to Tame and Wrangle Their Data* trends as #1 on Amazon under *Networking and Cloud Computing* category which I believe is a complex category to peak to #1. The book has around 60 practical implementation projects including machine learning and artificial intelligence. Our company also runs a book publishing company *High Performance Computing Institute of Technology* that publishes technology books for published and first-time authors as well.

I get huge response from people who read my blogs, books, eBooks, and they send me responses with their feedback as I've a feedback form available at www.gppulipaka.org and www.deepsingularity.io.

BIG DATA APPLIANCES FOR IN-MEMORY COMPUTING

A REAL-WORLD RESEARCH GUIDE FOR CORPORATIONS TO TAME AND WRANGLE THEIR DATA

DR. GANAPATHI PULIPAKA

SAP (Systems, Applications & Products in Data Processing) founded 46 years ago in 1972 even before RDMBS database was built officially. SAP gave commercial birth to many SQL databases as it generated such massive volumes of data. As of today, SAP still holds the Guinness World's record for building and operationalizing largest data warehouse in the world at 12.1 petabytes (PB). Today, SAP has 335,000 customers in more than 180 countries in the world with $27b revenues in 2017.

The key findings from the book:

Background of the Problem

- *The first time the term 'database' was coined to indicate it is portable to any machine.*
- *In 1974, the University of California at Berkeley built RDMBS product with (QUEL).*
- *Later IBM came up with RDBMS product System R with a structured English query language (SEQUEL).*
- *Microsoft built (MSSQL). During this time, RDBMS was shot to fame.*
- *In the 1980s, structured SQL became the standard query language for a large number of the RDBMS products.*
- *IBM introduced database two (DB2) as their robust version of RDBMS product.*
- *In the 1990s ODBMS was created.*
- *Subsequently, a golden digital era began with the advent of the Internet in the mid 1990s.*
- *Data grew exponentially due to online transactions.*
- In 1998, Mashey, a chief scientist at SGI presented a paper entitled Big Data and the Next Wave of InfraStress at a USENIX meeting.
- In the paper, Mashey discussed different data formats such as audio and video.
- Mashey presented exponential growth needs of data on physical storage systems and the needs to extract the data faster.
- Mashey discussed terms such as big memory and microprocessors, big net, bigger disk data, huge data, and technology change rates.
- In 2000, Lyman and Varian published a paper entitled How much information?
- Lyman and Varian discussed the information stored and processed by the population in exabytes per year.
- In 2007, EMC sponsored IDC for a data prediction research project.
- IDC published a white paper *The Expanding Digital Universe: A Forecast of Worldwide Information Growth through 2010* with the predictions of worldwide information growth through 2010.
- In this paper, IDC estimated that information would grow by six-fold to 988 exabytes through 2010.

Problem Statement

- The cost of managing computer generated data is very high with minimal rewards.
- Classical database RDBMS tools cannot provide real-time data access.
- An ever- faster, big data explosion is occurring globally.
- As a result, organizations are unable to make informed decision-making on time.
- Lack of access to critical data on time has critical impact on business decisions in an organization.
- Organizations need to analyze their transactional data that is integrated with real-time.
- Real-time integration is difficult with classical RDBMS tools running on ERP, CRM, SCM, PLM, and SRM systems.
- A deft tool is needed that can effectively process billions of records on ERP system.
- A big data tool is needed to provide integration with all ERP business applications.
- In sum, organizations need data in real-time to respond to the global needs of the business with faster analysis of data.

Purpose of The Research Study

- Most previous studies such as IDC have used a qualitative methodology to examine organizations with classical RDBMS database solutions.
- These previous studies did not conduct interviews or surveys with the participants.
- This can only be done through qualitative methods on organizations that were early adopters of in-memory technology solutions.
- The purpose of the study is to identity and resolve the global challenges of information delays in academics, aerospace, automotive, consumer products, food and beverages, government, healthcare, and utility industries.
- The objective was to analyze and present information with which to determine if:
- SAP HANA has diffused the big data via awareness, interest, evaluation, trial, and adoption.
- SAP HANA has efficient architecture to blend OLAP and OLTP compared to big data appliances such as Oracle and IBM.
- SAP HANA has shown promising results in revolutionizing emerging growth technologies such a mIOT devices and IVR.

Significance of The Research Study

- Findings can be used to explore SAP HANA's in-memory revolution research business cases.
- This study will add to the current research literature of in-memory revolution based on results.
- The study highlights how faster, bigger, higher performance of data can lead to more timely informed decisions.
- The study leverages surveys and interviews conducted at various client sites for high performance analytics.
- The study investigates perceived challenges, barriers, and successes in-memory implementation customers have experienced at various industries applying machine learning and artificial intelligence.
- Results also contribute to the body of research literature.
- The study develops performance benchmarks of SAP HANA against other big data technologies in the marketplace to distinguish the speed and efficiency.

Research Questions

1. How can SAP HANA speed up the diffusion of big data via awareness, interest, evaluation, trial, and adoption?
2. Why is SAP HANA more efficient than other big data appliances such as Oracle and IBM?
3. What data show that SAP HANA can shape the future of emerging growth technologies?

- A systematic study was conducted of organizations that have pain points with their business intelligence reporting, OLTP and OLAP.
- Challenges were voiced by participants of the survey.
- Solutions were proposed to solve their conundrums.
- The IDC research method implemented a predefined set of procedures.
- The methodology applied to this paper was based on the research conducted by IDC on behalf of SAP.
- The methodology was designed with highly structured methods including surveys with predefined questionnaires.
- The qualitative methodology was adopted by IDC on non-SAP HANA with web based surveys.
- The methodology involved qualitative study on organizations implemented SAP HANA.

Qualitative sampling

- The researcher leveraged a qualitative research methodology.
- The research analysis and qualitative sampling was to assess the secondary data from the IDC study and use methodology with new data on SAP HANA organizations.
- IDC survey involved IT managers and business managers with questionnaires.
- No permission to use human subjects for the study was required from the California University, Irvine Institutional Review Board pursuant to the U.S. Federal Government Department of Health and Human Services (2009) regulation 45 CFR § 46.1
- The study was based on secondary data and no human subjects were involved.
- The methodology of the IDC study was accurate and the results substantiated by the data collection and analysis.
- The IDC held interviews with various IT departments.

Qualitative data collection

- Gathered case studies from SAP by using the data to illustrate the advantages of having a single database.
- Gathered the data from a survey sponsored by SAP, with 759 participants of worldwide geographical composition.
- Administered web-based survey translated into four languages with 1,002 respondents worldwide.
- The extracted data from IDC survey results were applied to various industries to develop new SAP performance benchmarks with high-level fact-checking.
- The data was gathered from manufacturing, supply chain, logistics, finance, marketing, R&D, and customer service departments.
- These business functions represent the core of realistic SAP ERP, SAP SCM, and SAP CRM implementations.

Results

- SAP innovation center for SAP HANA partner Hasso Plattner Institute wrote a research paper in 2009 on blended OLAP and OLTP platform.
- In 2010, SAP implemented first-generation of SAP HANA in-memory database technology.
- SAP HANA implementation compressed database size for SAP from 7.1TB to 1.8TB.
- SAP HANA was the fastest product to diffuse big data and in-memory database platforms to several customers.

- SAP HANA gained strong momentum by implementing SAP HANA for more than 5,800 global customers and 1,850 SAP Business Suites.

Corporation	Prior to SAP HANA	After SAP HANA	ROI
Red Bull	1.5 TB database	0.3 TB database	N.A.
CIR Food	Reports required 20 minutes.	Few seconds	70%
Maple Leaf Foods	500 business analytics report	Reduced to 25 reports, running under a second.	N.A.

Molson Coors	Prototype reports required two weeks; delta data loads took 20 minutes, and required the use of a 4.6 TB Oracle database. Oracle database size of 4.6 TB	Prototype reports required one day, delta data loads took 2 seconds. ODS activations have shown 70% to 80% reduction in terms of time. SAP HANA database size of 900 GB. 80.9% of database reduction. SAP BW cube loading improved by 10 times.	N.A.

Frucor	N.A.	900GB SAP HANA database with a 511% of reduction in data compression ratio. BW queries ran 10-100 times faster. Data loads ran 5-10 times faster than before.	N.A.
Magazine zum Globus AG	Database size of 550 GB.	Accelerated data loading by 70% .	N.A.
SHS Group Ltd.	Database size of 661 GB.		100% ROI

Indust ry	Prior to SAP HANA	After SAP HANA	Implementation
Utilitie s	DSO activation – 21 Hrs 40 mins for 5.2 M records 4.3 TB database Query execution – 471 seconds InfoCubes population – 90 minutes	DSO activation reduced to 40 minutes 0.7 TB database Query execution – 1 second. InfoCubes population – 30 minutes.	SAP BW 7.3

Autom otive	N.A.	SAP HANA InfoCubes optimization – Improvement of 1.39 times	SAP BW 7.3
		DSO activation – Improvement of 4.15 times	
		Query execution time – Improvement of 8.5 times	
		BW Webi reports – Improvement of 11.6 times	
		SAP HANA InfoCubes response time – Improvement of 45 times	
SAP	Database size 7.1 TB	Database size 1.8 TB	SAP HANA

Lenovo	N.A.	Report analytics – Improvement of 20 times	SAP BW/SAP HANA
		Data compression – Improvement of 2 times.	
		SAP BW query performance – Improvement of 60 times	

Nissha	Batch processing of 7 hours Report generation – 346.6 seconds	Batch processing of 2 hours – Improvement of 71.4%. Report generation in 1.8 seconds – Improvement of 99.4%.	SAP BW/SAP HANA

Industry	Prior to SAP HANA	After SAP HANA	Implementation
Utilities	DSO activation – 21 Hrs 40 mins for 5.2 M records 4.3 TB database Query execution – 471 seconds InfoCubes population – 90 minutes	DSO activation reduced to 40 minutes 0.7 TB database Query execution – 1 second. InfoCubes population – 30 minutes.	SAP BW 7.3

Automotive	N.A.	SAP HANA InfoCubes optimization – Improvement of 1.39 times	SAP BW 7.3
		DSO activation – Improvement of 4.15 times	
		Query execution time – Improvement of 8.5 times	
		BW Webi reports – Improvement of 11.6 times	
		SAP HANA InfoCubes response	

SAP	Database size 7.1 TB	Database size 1.8 TB	SAP HANA
Lenovo	N.A.	Report analytics – Improvement of 20 times Data compression – Improvement of 2 times. SAP BW query performance – Improvement of 60 times	SAP BW/SAP HANA
Nissha	Batch processing of 7 hours Report generation – 346.6 seconds	Batch processing of 2 hours – Improvement of 71.4%. Report generation in 1.8 seconds – Improvement of 99.4%.	SAP BW/SAP HANA

Industry	Prior to SAP HANA	After SAP HANA	Implementation
Seoul's National University Hospital	Data extraction – 30 minutes for 3 – 6 years data Usage of third-line of antibiotics – 5.8% times	Data extraction – 1 to 2 seconds for 10 years data Usage of third-line of antibiotics – 1.2% and subsequently no third-line.	Microsoft BESTCare 2.0 and SAP HANA
Charité Universitätsmedizin Berlin	N.A.	Query execution – Few seconds on 20 TB database	SAP BW 7.3 and SAP BOBJ 4.1

Kardinal Schwarzenberg Hospital	Database size 760 GB	Database size 430 GB	SAP ERP IS-healthcare, SAP HANA
Mitsui Knowledge Industry	N.A.	Report analytics – 408,000 times	SAP ERP, SAP HANA, R, and Hadoop

Industry	Prior to SAP HANA	After SAP HANA	Implementation
City of Boston	Backlog of 600 pending permits.	Reduction of pending permits to 10.	SAP BOBJ
Fire and rescue NSW	Database size 750 GB	Database size of 220 GB	SAP BW 7.3 and SAP BOBJ 4.1
Honeywell Aerospace	Extraction of 5 TB – 12 hours	Extraction of 5 TB – Less than one minute	SAP BOBJ and HANA
Sagem	Database size 2.15 TB	Database size 443 GB	SAP BW

What are going to be the key developments in the industry in the next 12 months?

Machine Learning

Machine learning will be the most disruptive force of the future for the next decade with advanced distributed computing, embedded neural networks on FPGAs and ASICs system-on-chip architecture, with a class of neural networks and powerful hardware, insatiable network bandwidth to bring the machine intelligence to the society becoming the engines of mass production. The growth of big data increasing exponentially from petabytes to exabytes every year. Organizations need insights lead to positive actions providing the relationships among the data points. Biomedical, biotech, healthcare, particle physics, and genomics fields need breakthrough technologies to handle the performance issues while processing colossal amounts of big data. Knowledge breathes life into reporting dashboards from the mountains of big data. The research work needs high-performance computing and supercomputing to handle such big data that cannot be handled and processed through conventional computing methods through the x86 hardware era. The evolution of supercomputing introduced homogeneity in the clusters by wrangling the big data through high-speed processors, distributed computing, massive parallelization. The scientific field of handling performance issues grew year by year from processing the data in terabytes to processing exabytes of data. The data processing capabilities increased significantly from teraflops to petaflops. Supercomputing is at the inflection point with exascale computing architecture and advanced programming application models for parallel processing the big data through Hadoop and MapReduce paradigms to handle the performance issues stemming from the massive volumes of big data applying machine learning algorithms.

After traversing S-curve in the business and going past the Gartner's hype cycle year after year hitting the trough of disillusionment, IDC big data analytics research states that, the big data analytics market has shown a quantum leap of 11.9% through 2020 with expected revenues of $210 billion. Businesses started taking significant importance towards real-time analytics due to proliferation of smart phones, IoT, and extreme network bandwidth and exponential increase in hardware and computing power to process the data instantaneously. According to IDC FutureScape: Worldwide IT Industry 2018 Predictions 90% of Fortune 100 corporations will create new business models for revenue growth with data as a service models including the insights with data visualization and rich live data which will take the enterprises to the next level with 50% growth from 2017 year-to-year comparison. However, the big data setbacks with Cambridge Analytica and Mirai botnet hacks on IoT ecosystem took down 2.5 million IoT devices breaking customer regulations and data privacy laws in 164 countries originating from 49,657 unique IPs. According to McAfee CyberSecurity Research report, open source devices poorly secured with cybersecurity transformed by Mirai botnet into bots attacking worldwide targets. These setbacks can slow down the data as a service offering from large enterprises.

According to Gartner's research, artificial intelligence will fuel the engines of large enterprises taking the revenues to \$1.2 trillion in 2018 with a significant jump of 70% from 2017. Gartner also projects an ambitious \$3.2 trillion of AI value by 2022. According to Forrester Research, due to the lack of prototyping and expertise in the area of artificial intelligence 75% of early artificial intelligence disappoints due to lack of insights. The narrowed use cases presented for customers will not bring a potential benefit. The business leaders in the enterprises look to see the demonstrations of the working solution at some scale rather than always listening into the capabilities of what data scientists can do for the business. Showing the AI value require hands-on demonstration and proof-of-concepts inspiring the large-scale data scientists in the organization in TensorFlow, Python, Theano, Keras, and R.

The dawn of modern computing began when Alan Turing published a paper *On Computable Numbers* in 1936. In 1935, Alan Turing proved Central Limit Theorem as part of his dissertation. In the later years, machine learning gave the computing machines ability to learn from the data. Designing successful machine learning systems take the expertise to process big data at scale through distributed computing, cloud computing, supercomputing in high performance environments. Most of the organizations still take the advantage of applying traditional machine learning algorithms in Computer Science to resolve email SPAM, SMS SPAM, powering a number of advanced smart computing devices with natural language processing abilities such as speech recognition, conversational AI, self-driving cars, and defeating humans through chess or Go competitions. Supervised learning, unsupervised learning, and reinforcement learning still make large number of predictions for the enterprises about the future. Supervised learning applies machine learning algorithms to learn from labeled training data with known set of output signals. In unsupervised learning, when dealing with unknown data structure or unlabeled data meaningful knowledge and information can be extracted through data structure without the known outcome. Reinforcement learning can resolve interactive problems to improve the performance of the system based on the interactions with the environment. According to International Institute for Analytics, in a world of social media everyone claims to be a data scientist. Therefore, it is important to assess the skill set to ensure the enterprises can hire the data scientists to ensure a higher success rate for their big data analytics and artificial intelligence projects.

Deep Learning

According to Gartner, the rise of deep neural networks will bring a revolution and become the standard component of data scientists tool boxes in 2018. Now, running advanced hardware computing and technology stack with GPUs has fueled the Fortune 100 corporations. The cloud computing revolution will usher the economy by powering medium and small scale corporations with cloud-based deep learning without having to procure massive on premise data centers for data analytics and operating the businesses with higher efficiency.

A class of disruptive technologies in deep learning such as neural machine translation, quantum computing powered by deep learning, deep reinforcement learning with in memory computing, deep neural networks, convolutional neural networks, backpropagation, recurrent neural networks, generative adversarial networks, speech recognition, natural language processing, natural language understanding, natural language generation, data mining, text mining, and computer vision for IoT devices created a number of frameworks and libraries from AWS, Python, Torch, TensorFlow, Keras to resolve the complex conundrums with structured, unstructured, labeled, and unlabeled data.

Rapid advances in artificial intelligence achieved through deep learning by building an efficient neural language model over a billion words, which was never heard of before. This neural language model processes most complex big data as an input through directed belief nets with thousands of hidden layers to produce the output through fast algorithms. However, the conditional distributions through for each big data vector could be complicated due to the colossal amount of big data leveraging variational methods. As the number of parameters increases in an artificial intelligence framework, the system gets extremely complicated due to the approximations and conditional distributions. The neural networks of artificial intelligence have gained significant momentum in the recent times for processing enormous amount of big data for neural machine translations, speech recognition, and statistical language modeling. However, these computations are not only complex, but also CPU intensive. Building large-scale GPUs for deep learning have shown that processing large-scale big data takes incredibly longer time, sometimes a week. Therefore, the hardware architecture should be scalable with software architecture. Facebook artificial intelligence group has designed innovatory framework with softmax function for approximation with GPUs for training the neural network based language models with large-scale vocabularies. The adaptive softmax approach identifies the multiple linear dependencies in the large-scale vocabularies with the unbalanced distribution of the words and builds corresponding data clusters through natural language processing by minimizing the computational complexities. This adaptive softmax approach reduces the hardware costs and performance bottlenecks of the computations through matrix vector operations of natural language processing, thus significantly reduces both train and testing times. This tailor made approach suits best for GPUs when contrasted with earlier approaches of importance sampling, NCE, and hierarchical softmax that were purpose-built for CPU training and testing processes.

Facebook artificial intelligence group also developed a special open source library as part of Torch deep learning toolkit dubbed torch-rnnlib. This open source library allows developing newer recurrent network models and run those on GPUs for performance evaluation with minimum time allocated. The baselines can be attributed with cuDNN bindings. This is apart from the standard recurrent neural networks such as LTSM, RNN, and GRU. The benchmarks for such artificial intelligence framework processing colossal amounts of big data are measured through some standard benchmarks such as One Billion Word or EuroParl. These are complex training environments based on the large-scale size of the vocabularies that requires avoiding the overfitting and underfitting of the models through deep learning algorithms to perform a full-scale training with adaptive softmax on the GPUs. The benchmarks have shown that the processing capabilities are somewhat in the range of 12,500 words for each second a single GPU. This is a significant performance gain with high productivity levels of full softmax activation. This artificial intelligence framework and approach allowed the Facebook AI group to reduce the hardware infrastructure for big data processing through adaptive softmax approach with high accuracy.

The recurrent neural network in torch rnnlib allows defining several ways building the deep learning models with sequence-to-sequence learning for the variables with discretion of time with hidden Markov Chain properties. In other words, the future sequence is totally dependent on the current state of the recurrent neural networks for transition state. When Elman's recurrent neural network model is applied, it takes a[t] as the input and to produce an output b[t] and it also produces the past state of the recurrent neural network. It can be represented as
hs[t] = function(Z * hs[t-1] + C * A[t]),
B[t] = D * hs[t], where h is the internal hidden state of the recurrent neural network and function represents the activation of sigmoid function. However, GRU, LTSM, and SCRNN recurrent neural network are more sophisticated. One of the sophisticated models is language modeling. The language modeling is an artificially intelligent recurrent neural network that learns a large-scale distribution of the vocabulary with a sequence of words from a dictionary. The conditional distribution of the words is a product of joint distribution can be defined as follows in a language model.

PD(word[1],..., word[T])) = PD(word[T]|word[T-1],..., word[1])...P(word[1]).

This can be achieved with traditional approach by applying the non-parametric models with the statistical models. However, the latest recurrent neural networks are now renowned with parametric models for significant breakthrough of the language models with softmax artificial intelligent approach on a dataset of over one billion words. The torch deep learning framework developed by Facebook delivers number of APIs for generating recurrent neural networks. The LSTM, RNN, and GRU interfaces can be implemented when building the hidden states for processing large-scale big data. The interface rnnlib.recurrentnetwork can be leveraged for building large-size recurrent neural networks. The recurrent network interface from torch open source library can store the previous state of the neural network and sequence table interface can perform chain computations similar to what scan does. The method setupRecurrent by passing the language model and initialization function can setup the hidden states for the recurrent neural networks. During this process, the sequence table will feed each level of the cell on the recurrent neural network for building a new layer. The initialization function aids in constructing the hidden inputs. Few other modules and methods such as cell.gModule can be invoked to set up the recurrent neural network with LSTM model. The cell library within recurrent neural network has GRU, RNNs, and LSTM with pre-defined cell framework.

Once the recurrent neural networks are constructed these can be trained with large-scale big data on the neural network module interface by invoking the cuda function to run the process on the GPU. cuDNN can be invoked to boost the speed of the training significantly. The accelerated is observed almost twice the speed from the initial run of the recurrent neural network model. However, softmax function might take longer times particular for one billion word datasets. This example has shown how the hardware computations of the computers in combination with big data and faster deep learning algorithms can have significant impact of artificial intelligence on big data.

Data Science

The data science can be defined as *the convergence of Computer Science, programming, mathematical modeling, data analytics, academic expertise, traditional AI research, and applying the statistical techniques through scientific programming tools such as Python, R, TensorFlow, Java, on an ecosystem of SQL, NoSQL, GraphDB, streaming computing platforms such as Apache Spark, Apache Kafka, Apache Storm, Apache Nifi, Apache Flink, Apache Geode, and linked data to extract new knowledge discovery through data patterns and provide new insights from distributed computing platform from the tsunami of big data.* Though, many times it is possible to define the statistical language models, it's difficult to implement through object-oriented programming languages. Therefore, it is critical to wear the hats of an advanced programmer, infrastructure architect to provide web scale performance with in-memory computing and apply traditional research with machine learning and deep learning algorithms to create novel architectures unique to each enterprise and avoid one-size fits all approach. Real-time analysis is all the rage in the data science industry. Therefore, leveraging in-memory computing ecosystems can provide faster execution results to the corporations.

MemSQL is in-memory computing database engine that works as a processing engine for Apache Spark. Pinterest, a social network needs to identify the latest developing trends on their application intuitively based on what the consumers have pinned and shared the boards. Pinterest generates large-scale big data and number of real-time events. The events log contains number of pins and repins. The event data is transmitted to Apache Kafka. MemSQL in-memory database provides Spark connector. Apache Spark receives all the events from Apache Kafka through message queue for each event type including geospatial intelligence of the big data. The high-velocity data streams through Apache Kafka aggregating and filtering the event logs by event types. Apache Kafka generates the events at ultra-blazing speeds with high-velocity and high-volume big data. Apache Kafka works as a producer of big data. Apache Spark and Apache Storm work as consumers of big data ingest and process the big data by filtering the event type to update a number of database tables in MemSQL in-memory database. Secor is a log persistence service that writes the event logs to Amazon S3 as well from Apache Kafka. Hadoop clusters receive the data from Amazon S3 instances for performing the batch processing. Apache Kafka is a great tool for handling high-velocity and high-volume big data. However, Apache Kafka events and messages cannot be queried in real-time to understand and examine the patterns of the events for any particular queries triggered.

In Pinterest case, they leverage both Apache Hadoop and Apache Spark for different business reasons. For more than a decade Apache Hadoop has been the core of big data ecosystem as an open source ecosystem. Several corporations are still embarking on more Hadoop implementations across the globe. DNA sequencing and genomics require colossal amounts of area to store and batch process the big data. For healthcare organizations and genomics research Hadoop is still used to store and process large-scale big data on low-cost commodity hardware.

On the other hand, several organizations implemented Apache Spark requiring real-time data analysis with in-memory computing. In use cases, where the industries need to build recommendation systems for online systems that require near real-time processing and providing recommendations, they can implement Apache Spark along with Apache Hadoop for batch processing. Apache Spark is useful for energy and utilities industry to detect the consumption of electricity in real-time and perform load balancing and optimization of the electricity. For an industry like social media, both Hadoop with MapReduce and Spark are needed. Pinterest went for the implementation of both which was essential. Apache Spark supports a broader range of programming languages based on the organizational adoption of R, Java, or Python.

Several critical reasons cited for the organizations to adopt both Hadoop and Spark. At first, Apache Spark is new a replacement technology for Hadoop. Just like SAP HANA data in-memory computing processing engine and SAP HANA database are different. On top of organizations may not be able to accomplish batch processing, near real-time capabilities with Hadoop and Apache Spark, they also need an in-memory computing and high-performance database computing platform such as MemSQL, Aerospike, SAP HANA, IBM DB2 Acceleration, Oracle Exadata, or Exasol to store the events logs, system logs, and machine generated big data. There is large-scale of data generated from Medical Internet of Things in healthcare industry as well that requires such storage for tracking the epidemics through real-time processing and Hadoop for electronic medical records for internal operations. Apache Hadoop can add immense value to Apache Spark. Apache Spark processes the near real-time data that is generated on the fly, which is data-in-motion. Apache Hadoop stores historical data such as electronic medical records or historical social media data that can be batch processed, which is data-at-rest. Apache Spark and Hadoop complement each other, but do not replace each other. In-memory databases such as Aerospike or SAP HANA picks up the data from resilient distributed datasets and process it on DRAM without having to store or retrieve from the database. There are large-number of alternatives for DRAM memory, such as NAND or other flash technologies leveraged by IBM, Oracle, and SAP on their in-memory databases. Aerospike stores it on flash instead of on DRAM. Pinterest leveraged MemSQL in this practical implementation to store and retrieve the RDD data through DRAM. Pinterest is a project, where it has leveraged Apache Hadoop, Apache Spark, Apache Kafka, MLib from Spark library for machine learning algorithms.

Currently there are 500 organizations that have implemented Apache Spark and Apache Hadoop shows a compounded annual rate of growth at 58% through 2020 exceeding the market capital of $1 billion. As

artificial intelligence introduces advancements to enhance human life and not to replace, Apache Spark was designed to enhance Hadoop technology, but not to replace it. Most of the big data vendors such as Hortonworks, Cloudera, and MapR provide their data platforms with the entire stack of Apache Hadoop and Apache Spark together.

IoT

John McCarthy coined the term artificial intelligence in 1955 as a field of building scientific and intelligent machines. The Internet of Things has billions of data points scattered around the world with large-scale big data generated through smart meters, smart cities, sensors, and energy grids. The rise of the networks and integration with Internet of Things brings a new era of artificial intelligence with sensors capturing real-time big data for a wide range of industries. According to Gartner Inc, there will be six billion IoT devices by 2018. Therefore, artificial intelligence becomes the fundamental building block for building the strategy, process orchestration, methodology, and technology to analyze such large-scale IoT big data. IoT aggregates a tsunami of big data from the sensors and devices. The proliferation of sensors and devices is creating online explosion of continuous data streams with data-in-motion at colossal volumes. In order to sift through the billions of data points with intelligence artificial intelligence is required to find out the patterns through clustering algorithms and find the valuable insights. IoT used in manufacturing environments show the operational efficiency of the plants and regions where there is an association and correlation.

- Traffic incident management, traffic congestion monitoring and predictive analytics IoT systems.
- Large-scale IoT big data generated from biochips and pacemakers from the clinics and hospitals.
- Aerospace equipment maintenance predictive analytics through IoT sensors adopted by several corporations such as Rolls Royce, GE through Predix and Azure machine learning platforms with IoT event hubs.
- Smart cities create big data through IoT at astronomical scale.
- Smart homes create large-big data through IoT sensors connected to the home appliances.
- Autonomous vehicles create large-scale big data through IoT sensors and telematics.
- Agriculture field generates large-scale IoT big data, consumer electronics, and industrial IoT create big data through sensors.
- The transportation field carrying logistics generate the data through telematics attached to the transportation vehicles, GPS and various other devices apart from telematics generate IoT big data that gets uploaded to the distributed computing platform Hadoop or streaming platform for faster analytics and data visualizations through the artificial intelligent platforms.
- Retail industry uses LiDAR sensors and other monitoring sensors that generate large-scale IoT big data.
- Sports and fitness devices generate large-scale IoT big data through wearable devices.
- Telecom sectors generate large-scale IoT data through the sensors deployed across the world.

When such large-scale amount of big data is created, the traditional methods to write the programs as input and the output as the result of each task is quite complicated and time-consuming. The IoT data is rarely static and historical information extracted from enterprise data warehouses through regular methods is data-at-rest. Even reducing the sample size of the data through traditional programming cannot accomplish the results.

Therefore, sifting through such petabyte scale IoT big data is simply complex and requires training the labeled data on deep learning platform from the sensors and producing the output with data in-motion platforms with big data technologies such as Apache Kafka, Apache Storm, Apache Nifi, or Apache Flink. A combination of artificial intelligence and data in-motion analytics will be able solve the conundrums with IoT big data. Finding insights from continuous streams of IoT big data is challenging without implementing machine learning algorithms as part of artificial intelligence framework. Apart from applying the algorithms, the continuous streams of IoT are extremely fast and accelerated traveling with high-velocity and in high-volume. One of the reasons, why IoT big data requires faster machine learning algorithms and highly scalable computing platform with distributed computing without which the conundrums cannot be solved.

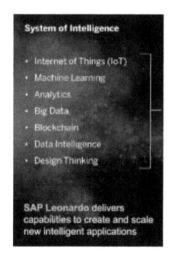

System of Intelligence

- Internet of Things (IoT)
- Machine Learning
- Analytics
- Big Data
- Blockchain
- Data Intelligence
- Design Thinking

SAP Leonardo delivers capabilities to create and scale new intelligent applications

Internet of Things

Use IoT technology to connect things with people and processes, and take advantage of the Industrial IoT and Internet of Everything (IoE).

Internet of Things ›

Machine Learning

Embed easy-to-consume machine learning capabilities into your business – and take advantage of AI-based insights.

Machine Learning ›

Analytics

Deploy analytics across your business to uncover better insights – and develop new processes and apps based on intelligence.

Analytics ›

Big Data

Connect to, process, manage, and store a wider range of data than ever before – from any source, structured or unstructured.

Big Data ›

Design Thinking

Get expert help with design thinking services such as solution ideation, rapid prototyping, and business case development.

Design Thinking ›

Blockchain

Embed blockchain services into your applications to speed up transactions and increase trust, visibility, and security.

Blockchain ›

Data Intelligence

Extract insights from a large network of anonymized data. Find ways to solve your business problems, monetize data, and more.

The only way to resolve the conundrums of large-scale big data generated by IoT devices, sensors, and telematics is through leveraging the last mile of IoT with artificial intelligence. Artificial intelligence can sift through the billions of data points created by IoT sensors and provide meaningful insights to the data through machine intelligence. Only when artificial intelligence can find the patterns and associations in IoT big data through clustering algorithms, there can be any solution for the decision process. Both artificial intelligence and IoT are complementary solutions. One cannot be without the help of the other. There are many advanced artificial intelligence applications for visualizing the large-scale big data analysis and machine learning predictive analytics through Microsoft Power BI and Splunk Analytics through machine learning for machine generated data from hundreds of IoT sources.

The artificial intelligent applications can put context to IoT data for providing inferences and provide meaningful insights through data visualizations. Some of the cognitive systems built by IBM Watson provide recommendation systems for continuous streams of IoT big data. There is potential promising future from the integrated artificial intelligence and IoT ecosystem such as SAP Leonardo for critical breakthroughs and challenges such as healthcare safety, the complexity of big data, and compatibility with integrated networks. SAP Leonardo will take the industrial IoT by storm in the next 12 months.

Cloud Computing, Distributed Computing, and HPC

One of my specializations in PostDoc in Computer Science Engineering is advanced big data analytics and machine learning in distributed and cloud computing HPC ecosystems. No doubt, currently it's the number one skill to likely get hired in 2018 from top 25 LinkedIn skills for 2018. A number of companies offer these courses such as Udemy that provides introduction to cloud computing, LinkedIn Learning offers Amazon Web services, storage, and data management, first steps towards cloud computing career paths and certifications. Coursera offers another course on cloud architecture, and edX offers another course on cloud computing applications which should take most of the beginners to start on a data science journey and become a data scientist to work on high performance computing environments such as CERN that performs massive simulations at Large Hadron Collider on AWS Infrastructure, NASA's Desert Research and Technology Studies (Desert RATS) that performs extreme cloud computing on robotic systems, extravehicular equipment for future missions in space with geospatial mapping and navigation techniques with communication systems in the field of Computer Science.

High performance computing is achievable through shared memory distributed programming. Shared memory distributed programming paradigm enables various tasks to communicate with each other by sharing the memory from different disk locations. In this model, the memory is shared and distributed across several locations of the disks at different memory locations. Through synchronization, multiple threads of a single process access the address space of memory locations by writing and reading to the same location. However, the synchronization mechanism also ensures the sequence of the read and writes operations in which various tasks may run into deadlock situations, as both the tasks might be looking to write to the same address space with the same key. Such contention of deadlocks to keep the integrity of the data can be accomplished leveraging locks, barriers, and semaphores. A semaphore operation can enable multiple distributed tasks with post and wait operations in queue. The lock paradigm performs lock and unlock operations to the specific shared memory address space to prevent simultaneous writing. The barrier works on task to prevent other tasks to process, till all the tasks reach the same point of event. MapReduce framework in Hadoop leverages shared memory distributed programming with a built-in function to handle distributed shared memory mechanism. MapReduce also provides a clearer storage layer for accessing the address space from any distributed cluster through shared-memory programming. MapReduce has the internal functions for synchronization and barrier between the map and reduce phases. HDFS natively provides the storage layer for shared memory distributed programming for the tasks to access the memory across HDFS.

In contrast to shared memory distributed programming, where the tasks share the address space for performing the write and read operations over distributed clusters on disks or memory locations, messaged passed distributed programming exchange communication through the messages. The limitations with message passed distributed programming particularly when processing large-scale data processing in cloud computing environment are memory overloads, data overload operations, and latency over the network.

The message passing distributed programming does not get the native support from the hardware of the system as the communication occurs through the messages. The standard specification of communication is from the Message Passing Interface (MPI) that transmits the message for both sending and receiving. Unlike, shared memory distributed programming, the message passing distributed programming requires programming to encode the functions for partitioning the tasks and exchange the communication of the messages in a specific pattern. Considering the location of the data is across the cloud-computing environment, the latency can be exponential when accessing the remote data lakes as opposed to accessing on-premise servers with localization of the data due to network latency and synchronization data points could lead into potential bottlenecks due to large-scale data processing. Both shared memory distributed programming and message passing distributed programming are insufficient to handle the large-scale big data natively in a cloud computing environment as they require either pre-development efforts in case of message passing distributed programming to exchange the messages in the environment and shared memory distributed programming require post-development efforts for replication or migration of the data. When there are large group of people accessing the data which resides in the critical sections of the memory, the contention for deadlocks increases exponentially along with the network latency. Also, in both cases, the distributed programs can introduce synchronous and asynchronous modes to process the data. In asynchronous mode, the data gets posted immediately without having to wait for any contention, thus improving the performance of the distributed tasks. However, it can cause potential issue with the consistency of the data in case of excessive data transfers. In case of synchronous programs, they introduce the barriers and locks causing delays on the performance of the system. However, it can significantly improve the consistency and integrity of the database. The other challenges in the development effort in a cloud computing environment required for both shared memory distributed programming and message passing distributed programming can stem from heterogeneous cloud environment. The heterogeneous cloud-computing environment deals with different operating systems, different network protocols, and different hardware computing environment, and the interfacing of multiple programming languages HDFS.

Analytics

Healthcare organizations need predictive analytics for providing quality healthcare and population health management. Building predictive models by applying machine learning algorithms is complex in the infrastructure-as-a-service or platform-as-as-a-service environments as it involves distributed computing. The emergence of predictive analytics in the healthcare industry has offered enormous opportunity to be able to predict the events in healthcare organization and other industries as well such as aerospace industry. Predictive analytics is a subfield of data science that deploys several multi-disciplinary fields such as statistical inference, machine learning, clustering, data visualization, and machine learning iteratively through the lifecycle of the data analytics. The stages can be defined as defining the problem statement for the organization, scope of the data analytics project, collection of big data, exploratory data analysis, data preparation, deployment of predictive models leveraging machine learning algorithms.

Definition of problem statement and scope

During the initial phase of the data analytics project, it is of paramount importance to understand the pain points of the business and the requirements before designing solution architecture for predictive analytics with machine learning. The business requirements should be defined during the data discovery phase and need to be translated into data analytics conundrum. For example, in healthcare industry, the healthcare organization might be looking for the epidemics and outbreaks in different parts of the world. The problem statement could be to predict the outbreaks based on translating the calls received by the emergency department and running deep neural networks to identify the speech recognition and geospatial intelligence to identify the impacted locations of the epidemic and the ability to predict the outbreaks based on rate of velocity, geographic location, and demographics.

Data collection

The data collection could be generated from disparate channels of data sources in both structured and unstructured formats. For healthcare organizations, the data might already be available in data lakes or data warehouses. However, it requires data extraction and loading from source format to target format as part of data collection phase.

Exploratory data analysis

Once the data migration, data preparation, and data conversion process is complete, the organization can explore the data to perform statistical inference methods, clustering, data mining, and machine learning algorithms and deliver data visualizations. The data still may not be in exact format for building the predictive models. In such case, data wrangling can be performed to build the data more accurately.

Development of prediction models

This is the critical stage to build the prediction models by selecting and applying a particular machine learning algorithm by building a predictive model. The datasets are divided into training and testing datasets. The training data is leveraged to train the model; the other partition of the untrained data is leveraged to test to determine the performance evaluation of the predictive model. The testing models can be iteratively run through a number of iterations with ensemble machine learning algorithm to avoid under fitting and over fitting and eliminating outliers and evaluate the machine learning algorithm that fits perfectly for building the prediction model.

Deployment of the model

The model can be deployed once the best fit for prediction model and performance evaluation is complete. However, there is reusability of the prediction model across multiple departments of healthcare organizations or other aerospace industry organizations. Such reusability of prediction model requires deployment through a web service and database across the organization throughout the nation or across the globe.

Azure Machine Learning

Azure machine learning is a Microsoft tool that runs on a distributed cloud-computing environment. The service can be run on browser.

The organizations do not require any additional hardware or software procurement for running Azure machine learning. Azure machine learning is also a data visualization service that enables drag and drop methods to build the prediction models and applying machine learning algorithms. Azure machine learning is an integrated environment from Microsoft. Azure machine learning service can pull large-scale big data from Hadoop ecosystem through Microsoft HDInsight and bring the data to Azure machine learning. Microsoft powered Azure machine learning through a number of algorithms as a result of Microsoft Research for various industries. Microsoft also leverages these algorithms to power their internal products such as Cortana and Bing.

Machine Learning Studio is part of Azure machine learning integrated browser-based development environment. In the recent times, Azure machine learning has created Azure notebooks to share the work from one department to another that is powered by open-source Jupyter notebooks on JuputerLab. Machine Learning studio or ML Studio allows visually creating the predictive models and performing iterations of training and testing data interactively. Pre-defined processes within Azure machine learning library may not cover all the scenarios. It may not be possible to find a drag and drop model for a particular scenario, in that case, the code can be written either in proprietary R language or in Python language and extend model with the developed code. ML Studio also provides access to query the data. The datasets can be simply be dragged and dropped in ML Studio environment to build an experiment and by submitting it to ML Studio with an algorithm, it can build the predictive model without code. Only when particular business logic needs to be incorporated with a machine learning algorithm that is outside the scope of already developed ML Studio, the code can be written in R or Python. The access to Azure ML Studio can be gained by subscribing to Microsoft account. The tool can be used by creating a machine learning workspace, assigning the workspace information, and workspace owner. Once the workspace is created, a machine learning page shows up. On the left side of ML Studio, a number of tabs will be displayed such as web services, experiments, datasets, settings, and trained models. In experiment, the statistical analysis or predictive analytics can be performed on the modules that encapsulate the machine learning library. Once the dataset is uploaded into ML Studio, it can work as an experiment module. Adding input and output ports can create a workflow. The input ports can have a single or multiple output ports. The procedure to create a new experiment would be clicking the new button, selecting an experiment.

Azure machine learning can be applied to aerospace industry as well apart from healthcare organizations. By creating an experiment to predict the delay of passenger aircraft with binary classification. The big data of historical information of the scheduled flight is collected in the first phase from United States Department of Transportation. The next step would be to perform some data wrangling by preprocessing the data through filtering to consider the most busiest airports in United States and a number of other attributes on each field. Once the final airport codes dataset has been wrangled and ready to be processed, another dataset for weather has to be prepared that has all the data attributes related to the weather conditions. Both the datasets need to be joined on Azure Machine Learning Studio and build the prediction model through Two-Class Boosted Decision Tree and train the datasets. For the purpose of comparisons, a Two-Class Regression needs to be selected as well, as this is a binary classification task. The results show the ROC (Receiver operating characteristic) with precision and recall parameters in addition to the area under curve. The results can be interpreted from the boosted decision tree model for analysis purposes. PowerBI on Azure platform can provide some rich and live data visualizations in real-time. Microsoft ($21.2 cloud revenues), AWS ($20.4b cloud revenues), and IBM ($10.3b cloud revenues) still lead annual revenue run rate for 2017. This shows that analytics and machine learning in the cloud will continue to rise for the next 12 months as more enterprises adapt the public clouds with more virtual machines running in the cloud.

Healthcare industry generates large-scale big data and requires business intelligence with data visualization analytics to monitor and improve the quality of the health. Decision-making is the core component of any industry. Business intelligence can turn the colossal volumes of raw big data into valuable information and key insights for decision-making. The business intelligence consists of data visualization tools, analytics, and process of data collection, extraction, transformation, and data analysis. The data visualization tools leverage business intelligence to extract the historical big data and compare with the current view of the enterprise from data lakes, data marts, and enterprise data warehouses. Some of the data visualization tools perform statistical data mining as well.

Tableau

Tableau has several features that can support healthcare industries through data visualization and analytics. The latest Tableau Suite can even perform k-Means machine learning algorithm on the dataset through automated built-in functionality. Tableau performs data integration between several departments of the healthcare industry and clustering of the big data. Tableau provides ease-of-access with drag and drop functionality by connecting to a disparate number of data sources from various departments of healthcare organization. Tableau can generate pace charts, pie charts, and bar charts and a number of reports in various formats for performing the analysis. The data visualization tool Tableau aided the organization to extract the data from various departments to analyze and support the patient healthcare, monitoring the diagnostics that led to the improvement of the healthcare operational performance and the decision-making. Tableau aided the organizations to quickly mitigate the costs, risks, and meet the regulations of HIPAA compliance. There is large-scale big data generated through the electronic medical records for HealthCare industry. Tableau data visualization tool can extract the electronic medical records and utilize the big data for decision-making and improve clinical outcomes for the hospital key performance indicators.

Prior to Tableau implementation, organizations are flooded with number of Excel spreadsheets, PowerPoint presentations with compiled summary data from Excel spreadsheets with pivot tables cause data inconsistencies and data integration issues. The compiling time will always be enormous. At times, the stakeholders of the healthcare organizations did not get the latest information for decision-making, as the historical data can be out of synchronization with the current data. Tableau implementation leads to systematic data visualizations of patients by each department in the clinic by treatment, emergency priorities, and readmission charts for the patients.

SAP BusinessObjects BI

McKesson Corporation is a healthcare pharmaceutical distributer and manufacturer of medical devices. McKesson also specializes in providing a medical billing and revenue management services healthcare IT solutions and built a special healthcare revenue management system for more than 20,000 healthcare providers across the globe with multiple specializations in healthcare field. McKesson chose SAP BusinessObjects BI as a business intelligence solution for building a self-service Revenue Management Solutions business intelligence suite with data visualizations for the customers to perform analysis on the data with big data relevant to each department. Most of the big data generated is from customer transactions. The data visualization tool SAP BusinessObjects BI provides reimbursement analytics. SAP BusinessObjects BI is a web intelligence data visualization tool that can on NetWeaver portal directly over the Internet. The solution also allows the customers to download 100s of generated data visualization reports based on the criteria defined in the selection of the report. McKesson also rolled out the solution to iPhones and iPads through SAP Mobility business intelligence to provide the data visualizations to the customers.

QlikView

QlikView is a business intelligence tool for many healthcare organizations that provides analytics through data visualizations. Sydney Local Health District has implemented business intelligence solution through QlikView data visualization tool. Sydney Local Health District conducts public health related research and provides biomedical, clinical services as well. Initially Sydney Health District had too many methods and tools for extracting the healthcare big data from various sources to build the reports. Sydney Health District wanted to build a platform to pull all of the data together into a single platform for the managers and clinicians. The deployment of Qlik Sydney Local Health District Targeted   Activity and Reporting System (STARS) business intelligence system has brought significant performance improvement to their system for efficient clinical decision-making, operational performance, and financial transactions. The data visualizations from Qlik also provided suggestions for customer-centric healthcare plans.

Business intelligence has an important role in healthcare industry that can offer instant actionable insights for decision-making. Healthcare institutions generate large-scale big data through pharmacies, laboratories, radiological units, clinics, financial systems, billing systems, reimbursement systems, and electronic medical records. The data deluge is in petabytes. However, the information to valuable insights is less. Every healthcare industry needs insights into clinical, operational, and financial key performance indicators. Therefore, healthcare organizations require business intelligence data visualization tools to organize all of this information into insights for decision-making process. The big data through data visualization supports population health management, quality of healthcare, cost reduction, and provisioning predictive analytics. A number of healthcare organizations around the world have adopted business intelligence and data visualization tools such as St. Luke's Medical clinic, Harvard Medical School, Columbus Children's Hospital, Blue Cross Blue Shield of Florida, Hartford Hospital, University Health Network, and International Federation of Red Cross and Crescent. The big data analytics, business intelligence, and data visualization tools have had a huge impact on healthcare industry. Following is a list of impacts with purpose:

Healthcare data privacy and consolidation of big data

Business intelligence data visualization tools provide a single point of access across the healthcare organization. Therefore, it introduces controls for the displays of the data for each department in the enterprise. Data visualization tools can introduce access level control policy for the healthcare organizations.

Optimization through efficiency

Most of the business intelligence reports through data visualization tools are ad hoc reports in real-time. They do not require to be scheduled to display the key performance indicators in the organization. The big data is displayed in near real-time and when the time gets updated in the collective big data ecosystem to provide real-time insights to the decision-making process.

Improved ROI

Healthcare organizations investing in big data platforms and moving away from traditional RDBMS systems are seeing immediate return on investments through cost reduction and monitor the credit and cash collection management and claims management of healthcare billing. The big data ecosystem and business intelligence also is expected to reduce the equipment cost of the laboratories, pharmaceuticals, prognostics, and cost of diagnostics.

Customer experience

Business intelligence improves the customer experience by gaining the insights into the customers through analytics and understand the customer insights through dashboards and analytics tools.

Improved healthcare

Business intelligence and data visualization tools are expected to improve the healthcare systems and quality of the healthcare by accessing large-scale healthcare participants' data generated through the genomics and demographics. The data visualization also aids the healthcare participants' data to blood transfusions and readmissions. The data visualization provides important charts and statistics that can be leveraged for immediate clinical decisions for healthcare. Some of the data visualizations from the clinical trials also improve the manufacturing costs of the drugs and bring the drug into the market at an accelerated pace.

Elimination of medical errors

Patient safety is another vital factor that contributes to the improvement of healthcare. Some of the clinical treatment options have high margin errors. Introduction of artificial intelligence coupled by the business intelligence tools with data visualization can improve the margin of errors and subsequently can lead to elimination of the errors. The data visualization tools can also augment the research methodology from the large-scale big data generated through clustering and k-means machine learning algorithm in Tableau business intelligence tool.

Key performance indicators

Business intelligence tools with data visualizations can aid the healthcare enterprises to obtain the key performance indictors through the dashboards and reports for improving the clinical quality and the utilization of the number of resources in the healthcare organization to measure the clinical performance and decision-making process through the big data. The data visualizations can also improve the practices of the clinics by identifying the trends for risk management. Business intelligence in healthcare organization can break down the data silos among multiple clinic practitioners, laboratories, and centers of diagnostics by fusing the data through data visualization with role-based administration. There are several outcome reports that can be built for healthcare organization such as cost effectiveness, clinical trial data, research program status reports, and the safety of the patients.

The key performance indicators for the patient can be delivered through data visualization tools of business intelligence for the global healthcare providers platform by integrating the patient care platform across hospitals under a network, laboratories, and pharmacies to support the evidence-based decision-making for the clinics. The data visualizations also help to perform the diagnostics of the patients and reduce the readmissions. Another important aspect of the data visualization through business intelligence tools is to support the financial key performance indicators of the healthcare organization. Similar to all the industries, healthcare also looks at revenue recognition for their financial operations. The financial operations are tightly integrated to the billing departments of hospitals, clinics, and pharmacies through the distributed cloud computing. The data privacy laws proposed by HIPAA recommendations also support most of the financial operations through the distributed computing network hosted in the managed services environment. Majority of the business intelligence tools can perform the drill downs on the budget forecasts of the healthcare organizations, cash flows, costs, and revenues. The analytical capabilities of data visualization tools aid the physicians to monitor the services and provide the reports to all the stakeholders. The data visualization tools in healthcare industry for the financial operations support accounts payable, accounts receivable, cash collections, migration plans of the customer and financial impacts, capital investments, capital expenditures, and cash flows.

If a brand wanted to work with you, which activities would you be most interested in collaborating on?

I'm highly passionate and would love to collaborate with brands in conducting webinars, podcasts, writing up white papers, eBooks, books, speaking opportunities, and product development.

What would be the best way for a brand to contact you?

The brands can contact me at www.deepsingularity.io or www.gppulipaka.org to hire me as a keynote speaker or interested in hiring me on a consulting project/product development in machine learning, deep learning, IoT, data science, analytics, and SAP projects. My contact information including phone number is shared at these websites. There's also a contact/feedback form. I provide a strong commitment by responding within 24 hours of the message with our next course of action or response to the audience who leave messages on blogs and books/eBooks.

REFERENCES

Aghaei, S., Nematbakhsh, M. A., & Farsani, H. K. (n.d.). Evolution of the World Wide Web: From Web 1.0 to Web 4.0. Retrieved April 3, 2016, from http://airccse.org/journal/ijwest/papers/3112ijwest01.pdf

Algorithmia (2016). Machine Learning Trends and the Future of Artificial Intelligence 2016. Retrieved April 30, 2017, from https://blog.algorithmia.com/machine-learning-trends-future-artificial-intelligence-2016/

Gade, K. (2015). Real-time analytics at Pinterest. Retrieved from https://medium.com/@Pinterest_Engineering/real-time-analytics-at-pinterest-1ef11fdb1099

Gantz, J., & Reinsel, D. (2012). THE DIGITAL UNIVERSE IN 2020: Big Data, Bigger Digital Shadow s, and Biggest Growth in the Far East. Retrieved April 5, 2016, from http://www.emc.com/collateral/analyst-reports/idc-the-digital-universe-in-2020.pdf

Gartner Inc. (2018). Gartner Says Global Artificial Intelligence Business Value to Reach $1.2 Trillion in 2018. Retrieved from https://www.gartner.com/newsroom/id/3872933

Grave, E., Chiu, J., & Joulin, A. (2016). Building an efficient neural language model over a billion words. Retrieved from https://code.facebook.com/posts/1827693967466780/building-an-efficient-neural-language-model-over-a-billion-words/

Hager, G., & Wellein, G. (2010). Introduction to High Performance Computing for Scientists and Engineers. Boca Raton, Florida: CRC Press.

IDC (2017). Big Data and Business Analytics Revenues Forecast to Reach $150.8 Billion This Year, Led by Banking and Manufacturing Investments, According to IDC. Retrieved from https://www.idc.com/getdoc.jsp?containerId=prUS42371417

Kowsari, K., Brown, D. E., Heidarysafa, M., Meimandi, K. J., Gerber, M. S., & Barnes, L. E. (2017). HDLTex: Hierarchical Deep Learning for Text Classification. Retrieved April 30, 2018, from https://arxiv.org/abs/1709.08267

Laskowski, N. (2015). Overcoming the big data bottleneck caused by data in transit. Retrieved April 5, 2015, from http://searchcio.techtarget.com/feature/Overcoming-the-big-data-bottleneck-caused-by-data-in-transit

Machlis, S. (2015). Most downloaded R packages last month. Retrieved from https://www.computerworld.com/article/2920117/business-intelligence/most-downloaded-r-packages-last-month.html

Patel, K. (2013). Incremental Journey for World Wide Web: Introduced with Web 1.0 to Recent Web 5.0 ? A Survey Paper. Retrieved April 4, 2016, from http://www.ijarcsse.com/docs/papers/Volume_3/10_October2013/V3I10-0149.pdf

Proove Biosciences (2017). World's Largest DNA Biobank And Big Data Set In Chronic Pain Surpasses Milestone Of 100,000 Specimens And 28 Billion Data Points. Retrieved from https://www.prnewswire.com/news-releases/worlds-largest-dna-biobank-and-big-data-set-in-chronic-pain-surpasses-milestone-of-100000-specimens-and-28-billion-data-points-300445273.html

Pulipaka, G. (2006). LinkedIn Profile. Retrieved from https://www.linkedin.com/in/dr-ganapathi-pulipaka-56417a2/

Pulipaka, G. (2015). Big Data Appliances for In-Memory Computing: A Real-World Research Guide for Corporations to Tame and Wrangle Their Data (2 ed.). Los Angeles, CA: High Performance Computing Institute of Technology.

Pulipaka, G. (2016). An essential guide to classification and decision trees in R Language. Retrieved March 8, 2017, from https://medium.com/@gp_pulipaka/an-essential-guide-to-classification-and-regression-trees-in-r-language-4ced657d176b#.gpgi2b97c

Pulipaka, G. (2016). Curse of Dimensionality- KNN Breaks Down: Part Two (With Code + Examples). Retrieved March 8, 2017, from https://medium.com/@gp_pulipaka/curse-of-dimensionality-knn-breaks-down-part-two-with-code-examples-82d48adc6b61#.jpms35tkg

Pulipaka, G. (2017). Applying Gaussian Na?ve Bayes Classifier in Python: Part One. Retrieved March 8, 2017, from https://medium.com/@gp_pulipaka/applying-gaussian-na?ve-bayes-classifier-in-python-part-one-9f82aa8d9ec4#.7ca6r69b9

Pulipaka, G. (2018). 3 Ways to Apply Latent Semantic Analysis on Large-Corpus Text on macOS Terminal, JupyterLab, and Colab. Retrieved from http://deepsingularity.io/3-ways-apply-latent-semantic-analysis-large-corpus-text-macos-terminal-jupyterlab-colab/

Pulipaka, G. (2018). AI Trained to Perform Sentiment Analysis on Amazon Electronics Reviews in JupyterLab. Retrieved from http://deepsingularity.io/ai-trained-perform-sentiment-analysis-amazon-electronics-reviews-jupyterlab/

Pulipaka, G. (2018). Building a Neural Net to Visualize High-Dimensional Data in TensorFlow. Retrieved from http://deepsingularity.io/building-neural-net-visualize-high-dimensional-data-tensorflow/

Pulipaka, G. (2018). Building Email SPAM Detector with Na?ve Bayes and AdaBoost Machine Learning Classifiers in JupyterLab. Retrieved from http://deepsingularity.io/building-email-spam-detector-naive-bayes-adaboost-machine-learning-classifiers-jupyterlab/

Pulipaka, G. (2018). Building SMS SPAM Detector and Generating a WordCloud with Kaggle Dataset in JupyterLab. Retrieved from http://deepsingularity.io/building-sms-spam-detector-generating-wordcloud-kaggle-dataset-jupyterlab/

Pulipaka, G. (2018). nstallation Guide for TensorFlow on macOS High Sierra 10.13.4 for your DeepLearning w/ Java, C, and Go. Retrieved from http://deepsingularity.io/installation-guide-tensorflow-macos-high-sierra-10-13-4-deeplearning-w-java-c-go/

Ray, B., Posnett, D., Devanbu, P., & Filkov, V. (2017, October 1). A Large-Scale Study of Programming Languages and Code Quality in Github. Communications of the ACM, 60(), 91-100. http://dx.doi.org/10.1145/3126905

Sterlin, T., Anderson, M., & Brodowicz, M. (2017). High Performance Computing (1 ed.). Amsterdam, Netherlands: Elsevier.

Sullivan, R., & Broszniowski, A. (2012). Big List Of 20 Common Bottlenecks. Retrieved April 6, 2016, from http://highscalability.com/blog/2012/5/16/big-list-of-20-common-bottlenecks.html

Turing, A. M. (1936). On Computable Numbers. Retrieved from https://www.cs.virginia.edu/~robins/Turing_Paper_1936.pdf

Turing, A. M., & Zabell, S. L. (2018, April 2018). Alan Turing and the Central Limit Theorem. The American Mathematical Monthly, 483-494. http://dx.doi.org/10.1080/00029890.1995.12004608

Ware, M., & Mabe, M. (2015). The S TM Report: An overview of sc ientific and schol arly jour nal publi shing. Retrieved April 30, 2018, from https://digitalco